DREAMER'S
DICTIONARY

DREAMER'S DICTIONARY

MAL THOMPSON

SUNBURST BOOKS

This book is dedicated to
Jake and Martina

This edition first published in 1995 by
Sunburst Books,
Deacon House,
65 Old Church Street,
London SW3 5BS.

ISBN 1 85778 153 8

Printed and bound in China

CONTENTS

INTRODUCTION

This book is designed to help the dreamer work out the meaning of their own dreams.

Hopefully, the information in this book will help the dreamer connect what they experience and feel in their dreams with what is going on for them in their daily life.

The function of dreaming is for the health and well being of the dreamer, and to aid the healing and resolving of some of the dreamer's inner conflicts. The world of dreams is a combination of the mysterious and the obvious. Dreams combine current events with memories from the past and include the emotions and feelings that go with them. Consequently the dreamer can be left very confused about what their dream means.

The following information and symbols are examples of dream language which the dreamer can use to interpret and work out the messages within their own dreams.

INTRODUCTION TO DREAMING

In our dreams the unconscious aspect of an event or an emotion is revealed to us as a symbolic image. The images or words that appear in our dreams often imply something more than their obvious meaning. They are referred to as symbols which are difficult to define or explain – sometimes they don't make any sense at all. To add to the confusion, along with these symbolic images is the occasional rational thought.

Dream symbols carry messages from the unconscious and instinctive parts of the human mind to the rational part of the mind. The unconscious takes care of the roots and the fine details of our thoughts, the bits we thought we'd dismissed. That is why everyday objects and thoughts can be powerfully significant in our dreams. Sometimes we can wake up seriously disturbed because the symbolism in our dreams contains so much psychic energy, alerting us to pay attention to it.

In waking life we all experience traumas, losses and difficulties from time to time. Sometimes the pain of these traumas is too much to bear and we don't allow ourselves to fully experience it. It isn't always the painful things that we don't fully experience. Most of us have busy lives, and so it isn't possible to take in every bit of waking experience. Our dreams do that for us. Our dreams sort out and sift through our experiences, combining recent memories with old ones.

Sometimes we shut away memories that are too frightening or disturbing. Through our dreams we make contact with those memories so we can understand them better. Dreams show the other side of the picture and contribute to our understanding of the whole of our potential. Dreams are always honest and they draw attention to what we need and desire. The unconscious seems to have our best interests at heart and through our dreams we make contact with our true needs and the roots of who we really are.

There are many types of dreams we can have which range from a sifting through of the previous days events to dreams that unblock powerful memories. Spending some time away in a different environment can often produce interesting dreams about life at home. Things are then seen from a another perspective, and can help the dreamer work out how they feel.

As dreams are unique to the individual, it is up to the dreamer to work out what their dream is telling them in relation to their life. To do this the dreamer needs to question themself and to be as honest as possible. Some interpretations are quite obvious, some are extremely obscure and hidden.

Most importantly, the dreamer's own interpretation will be the right one for them.

TYPES OF DREAMS

Daily Life Dream
These dreams contain the residue from the day's events with familiar people and surroundings. Emotions are always highlighted more than in daily waking life. The dream will point out the positive and negative aspects of the dream images and will help the dreamer confront their real life. Some things the dreamer won't want to face up to, recognise or accept.

Problem Solving Dream
There will be a hidden helper in this type of dream with an important message. It could be a person or a symbol. It is important for the dreamer to observe the character or symbol and remember what is said. The hidden helper could well be a personification of the self and could take the form of a complete stranger, a member of the opposite sex, a child or perhaps an animal.

Psychological Healing Dream
This type of dream can be very frightening, disturbing and powerful, with a nightmare quality to it. The dream helps the dreamer get through any difficult emotional blocks. Its function is to get rid of the part of the dreamer that is outdated, to clear away the issues and beliefs that the dreamer is holding on to unnecessarily and to make room for growth and change.

9

Some things that aren't resolved in waking life can be resolved in this type of dream because of the emotional intensity that is contained in the dream. The emotional blocks that were caused by the dreamer's unresolved problems are released.

Repeating Dream

This type of dream is similar to one where the dreamer is looking for something that is lost. If the dreamer remembers the same surroundings, people, symbols, feelings or messages in a dream, or the fact that something is being repeated then the unconscious is trying to say something. So what is it telling the dreamer? What is lost or missing?

The dreamer should find the thing they can least tolerate, to look at the dark side of themselves, the shadow side. The qualities and impulses the dreamer denies in themself are often the things the dreamer finds hard to tolerate in other people.

When this image occurs in a dream, the dreamer may hope for a breakthrough or a creative solution to their conflict. Some things are difficult for the dreamer to confront and it may be easier to invent psychological barriers to avoid facing something painful. If that happens, the dream will be repeated, or a particular symbol or image will be repeated. If the dream has a recurring theme or the dreamer finds themself again in a familiar place, they will know they have been there before. The emotional feeling will probably be the same. Perhaps the dreamer is avoiding something because it is frightening.

Lucid Dream

Lucid dreaming is when the dreamer knows during the dream that they are dreaming. These dreams tend to feel very real, the imagery is very vivid and intense in colour, feelings, sight, sound, taste and smell. Lucid dreams happen when a breakthrough or a connection occurs between the conscious and the unconscious. This connection opens up new possibilities for the dreamer to understand themself or others better. Lucid dreaming is very healing and enhances creativity, imagination and intuition.

Another element of lucid dreaming is that once the dreamer realises they are dreaming they can control what happens in the dream. It is possible to cultivate the skill of lucid dreaming and create situations that are pleasant or desirable, which can be of great benefit to the dreamer. Once this is established in dreams, the dreamer can then learn to achieve the same results in waking life.

Premonition Dream

If the dreamer is close to someone emotionally, it is possible to dream of having a conversation or confrontation of some kind with that person that actually does happen in the future. These dreams are usually extremely high in emotional content and precede a move forward either in the dreamer's relationship or in the dreamer's awareness of their own unconscious communication.

What the dreamer's unconscious or their intuition is telling them is usually true. That is to say, the unconscious creates a dream to bring to conscious awareness something almost expected. Remember, a premonition can only be a premonition if it comes true, otherwise it can be seen as a warning or a reminder.

Nightmares

These dreams always have a powerful message. Their intention is to draw our attention to something important, so much so that we actually wake up at the most intense part of the dream. It is important to understand and acknowledge what is so frightening to us after a nightmare. If the issue gets resolved, then the nightmares will stop.

Continuous nightmares, frightening dreams and disturbed sleep indicate that at a deep level there are issues that the dreamer's unconscious can no longer contain. When this happens, it is advised that the dreamer finds someone to share these dreams with. A counsellor or psychotherapist will be able to provide safe and expert help to the dreamer in these troubled times.

Dreaming Of The Dead

There are dreams where a deceased person appears to the dreamer and gives them a message or talks to them. Dreams of this nature can be very realistic and can convince the dreamer that the person was actually there. This kind of dream can be very healing and of great comfort to the dreamer. To dream of a ghostly presence of someone unknown, or someone who is threatening can be terribly frightening. Sometimes the ghostly presence can be a part of the dreamer's personality and sometimes it can be a real presence. The dreamer will know what is real for them.

When our dreams are obscure and weird and the images appear confused, it is likely that at a deep level the issues or conflicts have not been resolved. Sometimes we are aware of something important in a dream, yet we feel unable to reach it, we can't quite connect with it. Usually, the same issues will appear in a new dream and in a different form. The unconscious will always repeat something until we understand what it means.

REMEMBERING DREAMS

The purpose of sleep is not only to rest the physical body and the mind, it is to dream. A deprivation of sleep causes physical exhaustion, but if you don't sleep, you don't dream. Our thoughts, feelings and emotions are taken care of by our unconscious mind when we sleep. Lack of sleep deprives us of dreaming time so it isn't surprising that we can feel quite emotionally disturbed as a result of not sleeping enough.

Everyone dreams. Some people never remember their dreams at all, or they don't believe they are worth remembering. Most people remember their dreams sometimes.

We dream about every 90 minutes throughout the night. During this time there are changes in the heart rate and breathing patterns. There is a lowering of energy in the skeletal muscles which stops us from actually going through the physical motions if we dream about movement.

The level of arousal in the brain changes when we are dreaming so that we could actually wake up after a dream has finished. Normally we don't wake up unless it was a particularly powerful dream – most dreams are usually forgotten at this stage. Usually we go back to sleep until the next dream occurs. Most of us remember the dream we were having just prior to waking in the morning, but unless it was a very significant, it is soon forgotten.

Once you believe dreams are worth remembering,
then it is possible to work out your own way of
recalling your dreams. When you are falling asleep,
tell yourself that on waking up in the morning you
will give yourself time to remember your dream.

When you wake up, allow a few minutes to think
about what you were dreaming. If you rush out of
bed at this stage, any images will be forgotten.
Relax and let your dream images come back to you.
If you don't think too hard and force them, they
will come back more easily.

Don't worry if they are muddled or jumbled, just
allow yourself to remember as much as you can. As
well as the images, think how you were feeling in
the dream. Run through the dream once or twice
more, then write it down.

It does not matter whether you can remember a
complete dream or just a fragment. If you can give
five or ten minutes each morning to remembering
what was occurring in your dreams you will wake
up clearer headed and recall will be easier.

Sometimes we have difficulty remembering our
dreams because there is something frightening
about them and we don't always know what that is.
When this happens, try to admit your fear to
yourself and look at what it is you are afraid of.
The dream will come back to you when you have
looked at your fear in detail.

Dreams are our own creation and the characters or
objects in them are products of our imagination.

Sometimes it is helpful to draw the characters and events in your dream. Don't worry about trying to create exactly the same images, just relax, get in touch with your dream and draw whatever comes to mind. This will free you so that some of your unconscious feelings will rise to the surface. You can use colours that reflect the tone of your dream. Exaggerate if you want to. Create what you feel.

WORKING WITH YOUR DREAMS

As your dreams are unique to you, it can be helpful and useful to look deeper into their messages to find out more about what the dream is telling you. There are a couple of ways of working with your dreams to find out more. The first you can do on your own. Give yourself one hour only. Any longer simply loses impact and energy.

When you have written down your dream, look at the issues the dream raises and write them down. Remember these are your issues, your feelings.

What are the actions or inactions in the dream? What happens? How do these happenings relate to your personality and your behaviour? How do the attitudes, feelings and qualities of the dream characters show themselves in your personality?

Describe the conflicts and harmonies in the dream. Why do you think the dream has come to you now? What do you think the dream wants you to do? What would you like to avoid? How does your dream relate to other dreams? Write down the dream symbols or objects in the dream. How does your dream relate to your feelings in waking life?

When you have answered these questions as honestly as you can, try talking to one of the dream characters. You can do this out loud, or in your head. Ask all the questions you need to know the answers to. Find out what you want to know. The answers will come if you let them; usually the first response that comes into your head is the right one. Keep going, let it flow until you have worked on your dream for an hour. Then stop. Give yourself a little break of about 10 minutes, then have a look at what you've found out.

The most important thing is to remember the feeling you had in your dream. Find the feeling and then look back over your life and remember the last time you had that feeling. What situation evoked that particular emotion?

Try looking at your dreams with a partner. Talk about the dream as if it were occurring in the present tense. Try being one of the symbols. For example, 'I am a green chair.' Discuss your feelings as a green chair. What do you represent? What do you want from the other dream symbols?

You create everything that comes into your dreams. If you relive the characteristics you have projected onto your dream symbols, then you will understand their reality in relation to your own personality.

Having identified with some of the dream characters in your dream, imagine that they could talk to each other. First take one role and speak to the other one, then switch roles and reply with speech or a gesture or whatever feels appropriate.

Allow a dialogue to develop, let it flow beyond the dialogue that occurred in your dream. That way you will see a connection between this dialogue and what is happening in your life.

Dreams contain the projected parts of yourself that you don't always want to own, the parts of yourself that you don't like. Dreams represent whether or not you are at peace with yourself. They show you your conflicts and your difficulties. They have many meanings and you can work out your own interpretations. They tell you how you really feel. Sometimes the answers to old conflicts become obvious. If you see yourself more clearly then it becomes easier for you to make decisions and to know what you really want.

It takes time and practice to work on your dreams. Some things take a long time before they are resolved. Don't worry if you misunderstand your dreams or you get it wrong because important themes always repeat themselves.

You could try an experiment and 'ask' for a dream before you go to sleep. This can be very helpful if you are feeling stuck by a problem or conflict. As you are falling asleep, ask your dreams to help you by giving you an answer. Find a way of asking a question and repeat it several times as you are falling asleep. Concentrate on it for as long as you can. The answer in your dream may not be obvious, but there is a good chance that something in a dream will be connected to your current conflict, and you may wake up with changed energy which will inspire you to try something different. Good luck!

THE DICTIONARY

Abandoned To be abandoned in a dream signifies that the dreamer needs to get in touch with feelings of loss, to grieve for what has been lost. To abandon someone or something suggests that the dreamer may have a desire to let go, to move on a step towards something new.

Abduction If abducted the dreamer needs to look at who is abducting them, what this person means to them and how they are letting the abductor restrict them in their life. To abduct someone else suggests that the dreamer wants someone or something they cannot have. To witness an abduction suggests that the dreamer feels out of control in their life.

Abortion Perhaps the dreamer wants to get rid of something or someone. The dreamer could be grieving for what has been lost – a lost child or childhood. The dreamer's feelings about abortion need to be examined.

Abroad The dreamer needs to ask themself, 'Where do I want to be, who do I want to be with or get in contact with?'

Abyss This is life's darkness, life's bottomless pit and symbolises the fear of the unknown. What or who does the abyss represent for the dreamer? An abyss can represent the dreamer's darkest fears, the shadow side of their personality.

Accelerator This reflects the dreamer's need for things to move quicker in their life. Is the dreamer pushing themselves or being pushed? How does it feel to be moving fast? What is the dreamer avoiding in their need for speed?

Accent To dream of accents implies a dream of language and communication. How does the accent sound to the dreamer? How does the dreamer communicate with others? Do some things sound 'foreign' to the dreamer? If the dreamer is talking with a different accent or in a language which is foreign to them, the dream is telling them that they have the power to communicate, even if they do not think so.

Accident The unconscious is telling the dreamer what they already know: that accidents cannot always be prevented and that they may need to examine some of the accidents that have happened in their life, as well as their fear of 'What might happen if . . . ?'

Account How does the dreamer feel about money and taking responsibility for their own life? This kind of dream can indicate to the dreamer how they feel about paying what is owed and what they feel they deserve for themself.

Ace The significance of any dream involving cards, either playing cards or Tarot cards, depends on the dreamer's feelings about what the cards mean for them personally. As a rule, the Ace itself signifies the number one, a fresh start, growth of some sort. It can also symbolise the dreamer's feelings about card playing, winning or losing, gambling, luck, and how they play the game of life.

Actor/Actress What role is the dreamer playing in their life? Is the dreamer playing a role or are they being true to themself? The appearance of someone famous in a dream can point out a person the dreamer identifies with. What message is the actor giving the dreamer?

Adultery A dream about being unfaithful to a lover can signify a desire for someone else to fulfil a need not being met in a current relationship. If the dreamer dreams of their partner being unfaithful, this can indicate doubts about the relationship. The dreamer needs to be aware of their own feelings in the dream. *See also* Anima and Animus.

Africa The Dark Continent can represent the shadow, something from the unconscious not yet revealed or a desire for a different experience. What does Africa mean for the dreamer?

Aggression Strong emotion felt or expressed in a dream tells the dreamer of their real feelings. Feelings of aggression, anger or rage are there for a reason – survival against whatever the dreamer feels threatened by.

Air The unconscious feels there is something in the air for the dreamer. What is the quality of the air? What does it feel like? Smell like ? Look like? Does the dreamer want to breathe it in or blow it out? Is it clean air or cloudy air? The answers will give a clue to the dreamer what that something is.

Airport What is the significance of airports in the dreamer's life? Does the dreamer feel they are arriving at something in their life, or leaving something behind? Both signify a change of some kind in the life of the dreamer.

Alcohol The dreamer needs to look at how they feel about alcohol in relation to themself and the people in their life. Is the alcohol used or abused? What are its effects? How does it change things and what happens?

Alligator To dream of an alligator may be the unconscious pointing out to the dreamer something hidden or below the surface. It shows the need to be alert to what could happen. The dreamer should be aware that they need a time of clear communication.

Altar An altar is traditionally a symbol of self-sacrifice. The dreamer needs to look at what the benefits are for them in sacrificing something, or perhaps being a martyr. What does the dreamer really want for themself?

Amazon The second longest river in the world can signify for the dreamer their flow of life. Is the river flowing smoothly or dangerously? The Amazon can also personify strong intellectual qualities in a woman, the female warrior type. *See also* Anima and Animus.

Amber This orange-coloured stone which originates from the shores of the Baltic has healing qualities. The colour amber in relation to traffic lights is in between stop and go. Perhaps there is some relevance in the dreamer's life to this in-between position.

America The significance depends heavily on the dreamer's personal associations with America, how they feel about America in general and whether they have a desire to go there. 'The American Dream' stands for democracy and equality. Does the dreamer want something better for themselves?

Amethyst This stone was thought to be a remedy for intoxication, and so signifies the dreamer's desire for comfort and peace of mind.

Anchor This may signify a feeling of being held back, or a need to be grounded in some way, reflecting a desire for stability or being held.

Anima The anima is the feminine aspect of the dreamer's personality. In dreams it appears in many archetypal forms. In a man his female side can appear as an alluring woman to show him the feminine within him. This can be confusing to the dreamer, begging the question, 'Is this another person or part of me?'

Animal Our connection with animals starts in childhood by imitating their behaviour and characteristics or making friends with them. Most people identify with animals in some manner and want to communicate and get some response from them. Our fascination with animals stems from the characteristics they are given in childhood stories and what they mean to us. Most fairy tales include a cunning fox or a protective swan or a monstrous beast that hunts and devours.

Throughout history ancient tribes used animal spirits or totems to guide and protect them. Each animal represented a particular ability or strength.

In dreams animals appear as symbols of human behaviour and characteristics with important messages about how the dreamer is using the energy related to that particular animal and how the dreamer feels about their own animal instincts.

Some of these animal symbols are interpreted from the ancient American Indian totems and the medicine teachers. Their value is in the healing of mind, body and spirit. The animals that appear in dreams connect the dreamer with the essence of that creature. As whatever appears in a dream is created from the unconscious, the dreamer can assume that the character of the animal is a part of their personality and they can own it.

How the dreamer treats an animal in their dream gives vital clues to the message the dream is trying to convey and can reveal a great deal about how the dreamer has been treated. Trying to control the animal signifies trying to control the dreamer's instincts. Killing the animal is a sign that the dreamer is trying to destroy part of what they are. To eat the animal signifies the regeneration of the energy associated with it.

Baby animals signify that the dreamer is in touch with their own vulnerability or their reluctance to grow up or to face life. This dream highlights the need to be protected, cared for and taken seriously. Wounded animals put the dreamer in touch with their own wounds.

To be attacked by a wild or dangerous animal warns the dreamer that there are dangerous instincts within or people around them that are dangerous. The instinct or drive may be harmful and suggests the dreamer may want to abuse or destroy themself. If the dreamer is very dependent on someone, the unconscious compensates for this by making them appear in their negative form, symbolising the dreamer's fear of losing that person. *See* individual animals for their meaning.

Animus This is the masculine aspect of the dreamer's personality. We all have male and female energy within us. A dream showing the dreamer their animus will be the masculine displayed in a powerful form. We need the balance of masculine and feminine energy within. The dreamer will feel a strong attraction to the archetypal image their unconscious is showing them. It will feel powerful and will be seen clearly.

Ant Ants symbolise that slow, steady progress and patience is needed by the dreamer. The dreamer must trust that help or reward is possible. The ants also symbolise cooperation and industriousness.

Antique This symbolises connections with the past, family history, childhood and relatives. The dreamer should examine what value they place on issues in their life.

Anus The anus is a representation of the feelings that the dreamer releases or holds on to. It can symbolise letting go and also how the dreamer gives of themself. This dream may be highlighting basic feelings and babyhood feelings of pleasure.

Ape/Baboon Primitive, regressive and aggressive tendencies displayed in a dream give the dreamer some message about someone's behaviour. Apes or baboons also signify copying or imitating.

Applause This dream could point to a need for praise and recognition either from others or from the dreamer themself.

Armadillo To dream of armadillos symbolises the need for boundaries. Is the dreamer aware of where they stop and someone else begins?

Arm Arms represent the dreamer's ability to hold, give, take, love, create, defend and reach out. Is the dreamer trying to keep someone at arm's length or trying to welcome someone with open arms?

Army The dreamer's associations about being in a group or belonging to a group need to be looked at. What would being in the army mean for the dreamer? It could be about war or fighting or about the camaraderie and rapport that grow between members of a group when they are under extreme pressure or stress.

Attic This is a symbol for the spiritual side of the dreamer's nature. Their deepest feelings and their highest aspirations are shown in this dream.

Australia Depending on the dreamer's personal associations with Australia, dreaming about this large island between the Indian Ocean and the Pacific Ocean would indicate that the dreamer's unconscious is telling them to look perhaps at things from a distance. How would the dreamer feel about being that far away?

Autumn After the richness of summer comes the slow end. The harvest of the produce of summer is followed by decay. Autumn shows that all good things must end, die or rest. To dream of the autumn signifies maturity and the acceptance of endings. It reminds the dreamer to reap what has been sown before it is too late.

Awake To dream of waking up while still asleep means that the unconscious is telling the dreamer to be awake and alert to the particular message of the dream they are having.

Baby This could be part of the dreamer's 'baby', telling them something about their very early life. Perhaps it shows a desire for a baby, something to look after and nurture. It could reflect the dreamer's need to be looked after, or promise something new for the dreamer, a new idea or way of life. *See also* Birth.

Back To see the back of something or someone in a dream is telling the dreamer that they need to look at things from a different perspective. How important is the back view? Looking back at the past might be helpful. Because of the backbone running its length, it often signifies strength. The dreamer may also feel that someone is trying to dominate them, culminating in a 'Get off my back' feeling. The lower back symbolises the dreamer's feelings about support.

Badger The badger symbolises strength, hard work and the need to recognise that aggression and anger are sometimes necessary for the dreamer to feel understood or recognised.

Baggage Baggage is a symbol of important and heavy responsibilities. How much baggage is the dreamer carrying, either for themself or someone else? How does the dreamer feel about this load?

Baker/Baking The dreamer's desire for everything to 'turn out alright' is symbolised by baking. If the dreamer is having these sort of dreams then the situation probably will resolve itself.

Balcony To be on a balcony or ledge, looking at a view, suggests that the dreamer is content about what they are seeing. If the dreamer feels scared or unsafe, this will reflect how the dreamer feels about some aspect of their life.

Baldness What is the dreamer afraid of losing? This may not just be a dream about hair, it could be about losing many things.

Ball This shows the wholeness of something, completion. Is it a large or small ball? Was it being played with? Was it a game?

Balloon Something fun, floaty and colourful is symbolised. However, the significance depends on what balloons mean for the dreamer. This may be childhood parties and festivities, or the fear of it bursting and being gone.

Bank The dreamer has invested in something, either emotional or practical. Perhaps it is a symbol for their 'wealth of experience', their memories. Can the dreamer draw on their experience? How secure does the dreamer feel in relation to what is happening in their life?

Barefoot To walk barefoot signifies the dreamer's desire to touch on what is the truth for them, enabling the dreamer to get in contact with their feelings. The dreamer may need to expose these feelings, or may need to tread carefully, depending on the surface they are walking or standing on.

Bat Death and rebirth are symbolised by bats. To dream of bats shows the dreamer's need to let go of old habits or patterns and make way for the new.

Bath This symbolises the dreamer's need to wash something away.

Bazaar The dreamer has many different things going on. What are the choices in the dreamer's life? Will they get a bargain or be ripped off? How the dreamer feels and what they do at the bazaar need to be looked at carefully.

Beach The import depends a great deal on what associations the dreamer has with beaches. Is the beach in the dream sandy or rocky? Is it warm or cold and windy? Is it peaceful or crowded? How does the dreamer feel on the beach? Perhaps it symbolises the dreamer's need for fun and relaxation, solitude or peace and calm.

Bear The need for introspection or silence to find other levels of consciousness or imagination is symbolised when the dreamer dreams of bears. Bears symbolise the mother or the womb, a safe place for hibernation and thought.

Beard What is the beard disguising? What is really there underneath the beard and how different would things look in the dreamer's life if the disguise or cover up were removed?

Beaver A beaver in a dream symbolises that it is time to put plans into action or to complete something. The dreamer must look for alternative solutions to problems and protect what they have already created and put their energy into.

Bed A need for solitude or retreat is symbolised. Protection and sanctuary are required. There is a need for escape from difficulties.

Bee Qualities such as industrious, hard-working and hidden sweetness are symbolised by the bee. However, when bees are attacked they sting. Perhaps the unconscious is telling the dreamer to stand up for themselves.

Beggar Who does the beggar signify for the dreamer? It could be how the dreamer sees themself in terms of feeling deprived in some way. The dreamer's unconscious may be telling them that they are depriving someone else of something.

Bell This is a reminder to the dreamer of something important. Something or someone may have been overlooked in the dreamer's waking life.

Bible The dreamer is searching for answers. Dreaming of the Bible shows a need for help and advice. Depending on the context of the Bible in a dream, it symbolises that the dreamer has all the answers inside them.

Birth Dreams about birth are very powerful in their emotional content. To dream of giving birth indicates a new aspect of the dreamer's personality is emerging, something that has been hidden or unexpressed or undeveloped. If they dream about being born, it suggests a need for enlightenment or renewal. It indicates hope and that escape from present difficulties is possible. Giving birth to strange objects indicates the expulsion or rejection of unwanted issues in the dreamer's life.

Black The colour black is associated with death and mourning – with fear. It highlights the dreamer's feelings of being trapped or stuck. It can point to something hidden from view, a lack of vision or lack of clarity. This depressing colour symbolises the dark part of the unconscious.

Blind To dream of being blind indicates that the dreamer has lost sight of or is unclear about something. Maybe the dreamer is feeling lost.

Blood If the dreamer is bleeding, the message is about pain. Something is hurting the dreamer, but do they know what it is about? To lose a lot of blood in a dream suggests something is depleting the dreamer of their energy. Seeing blood could reflect the dreamer's anger about something.

Blue The colour blue symbolises the dreamer's need to find spiritual understanding and inner truth. Feelings of gentleness, compassion, peace of mind and forgiveness are evoked by this colour. Blue can be liberating for the dreamer who is impulsive and acts without thinking, or the dreamer who has become resistant to change.

Bodiless To dream of being bodiless indicates that the dreamer feels unrecognised or unnoticed. The dream may be pointing out their loneliness. They may be cut of from their feelings or their sexuality.

Body Our physical body refers to our sense of identity and represents physical life. We feel our emotions in our body, and so the body becomes a vessel for our locked up feelings.

Not only do we use our bodies consciously, most of us have an acute awareness of how we feel about our bodies. Our bodies respond to our unconscious feelings, so some of us develop eating disorders or abuse our bodies with drugs and alcohol. Often people that are very large become so because of a subconscious need for protection of some kind.

We use parts of the body to express our feelings, for example, 'They get in my hair,' 'I can't stomach this any more,' and 'They make me sick.' These are all symbolic expressions which describe feelings. Because of this, dreaming of different parts of the body can give the dreamer vital clues about how they feel and can assist them in connecting their emotional life to their physical life.

To dream of an ache or a pain, or a part of the body that is injured or diseased symbolises the dreamer's fear of illness or being incapacitated, handicapped or fatally ill. The dreamer may fear some kind of loss of control. It also symbolises the need to express the pain or the emotions relevant to the part of the body that has been highlighted in the dream state.

To dream of the top half of the body represents the thinking and feeling states, the lower half the sexuality and instincts. To dream of one part of the body without the other indicates that which is missing in the dreamer's life. *See* individual parts of the body for their meaning.

Book Books reflect something unknown or hidden, perhaps a question. Maybe they symbolises memories. The dreamer's life story is unfolding.

Boot New boots signify a chance to start afresh in some area of life, or new a choice for the dreamer. Old boots indicate a situation that is comfortable and safe, but for how long?

Borrow To borrow from someone suggests a need for help. What is happening with the dreamer's own resources?

Box Depending on the circumstances, a box can indicate issues around containment. Has the dreamer hidden something or do they need to take something out of the box and look at it?

Brake This indicates the dreamer's need to stop and look at what is currently happening.

Break The meaning of this depends on what is broken and how the dreamer feels about it. It signifies the end of something for the dreamer.

Bridge This signifies a connecting link between two situations, and that a period of transition is needed while the dreamer decides what to do.

Buffalo To the American Indians a white buffalo signifies that prayers have been heard and a time of abundance is to come. Buffalo also symbolise the sharing and acknowledgement of the harvest.

Bull A bull seen in dreams is a symbol of stubborn pride and great power that defends vulnerability.

Burglar The burglar is a person that the dreamer wants to keep at bay, someone they feel intrudes on them in some way.

Bus Travelling on a bus suggests a desire for companionship and anonymity. That is, the safety of being with others without being too exposed.

Butcher This dream strongly indicates anger and aggression. Who in the dreamer's life is performing the slaughter?

Butterfly The dreamer feels something in their life is elusive and intangible. This could be a childhood feeling or memory urging the dreamer to get in touch with who they really are. To dream of a butterfly can also symbolise a transformation for the dreamer. Which stage has the dreamer reached in their life-cycle: the egg stage – an idea in the dreamer's mind; the larva stage – the decision based upon that idea; the cocoon stage – making that idea a reality; or the birth stage – the sharing of the completed idea?

———

Cage Some area of the dreamer's life is inhibited and restricted. They have a feeling of being trapped. What or who does the cage represent for the dreamer?

Cake The dreamer may feel a need to enjoy themself and taste some of the sweet things life has to offer. They may be tempted by something they know they cannot have. Alternatively, the dreamer may have been too indulgent, and so their unconscious is pointing this out.

Camel The camel, when it appears in dreams, symbolises endurance. The dreamer must look at how they get through their difficult times, as the unconscious is trying to tell them something about the way they do this.

Camera The dreamer needs to capture or hold on to something important. What in the dreamer's life is the camera representing?

Cancer The dreamer's fear of death or illness is represented by cancer. This dream can indicate something that is sapping the dreamer's energy. The dreamer needs to focus on what is no longer wanted in their life.

Candle This symbolises something or someone important to the dreamer. It can be a memory or a reminder of something special.

Car What or who is the driving force in the dreamer's life? Is the dreamer driving themselves or is someone driving them? How does the dreamer feel in the car?

Cat The unconscious is telling the dreamer to use their intelligence and intuition to help themself.

Cave This represents the unconscious and a desire to return to the womb – a safe place, a hiding place from the pressures of life.

Cell The dreamer has fears of imprisonment, or is feeling trapped or powerless. This indicates the dreamer's feelings of isolation about something in their life.

Chain Depending on the context of the chains in the dream, chains usually remind the dreamer of their strong link with something or someone. How important to the dreamer is that link?

Chair If the chair is empty, it shows a vacancy. Something or someone is missing in the dreamer's life; perhaps they have lost something.

Chase What or who is the dreamer running away from? It could be an aspect of themselves that they don't want to address, or a fear of the recognition of the truth. If the dreamer is doing the chasing, the dream indicates an urgent need.

Chest Like the stomach, the chest is a part of the body where emotions can be withheld, particularly around the heart. The dreamer needs to examine what feelings are held there. Does the dreamer's chest feel heavy or light?

Child This can symbolise the dreamer's inner child. It is important for the dreamer to observe and be aware of their feelings in relation to the child or children in the dream. It can indicate the dreamer's childhood feelings which will still be inside them.

Choke To choke in a dream symbolises bottled up feelings that are trying to get out.

Church Depending on the dreamer's feelings and religious beliefs, a church symbolises a place of safety and approval.

Clothing Clothes signify image, façade. It is important for the dreamer to note how they felt in the clothes they were wearing in the dream. Does the dreamer want to cover something up or to have a different image or disguise?

Cobweb The dreamer's unconscious is telling them that they might be seeing things as more complicated than they really are. Alternatively, the dream might be saying there is more to a life situation than there is on first sight.

Coffin A coffin symbolises anything to do with death: the death of a situation, the death of certain feelings or the death of a particular way of being. It indicates to the dreamer that they might feel there is no escape from what is currently happening in their life.

Colour Researchers have argued for years about whether we dream in colour or in black-and-white. What is more important is whether the message the dream gives the dreamer is about the relevance of a particular colour. If a particular colour is highlighted then the dreamer is meant to notice it and work out what it means for them.

As we look around us, everything we see reflects colour. Colour and shadows define the form and shape of everything we see. Hence, using colour to understand dreams has been used successfully for thousands of years. Colour is used to understand the essence of energy.

We are a series of energy fields which are affected by the constantly changing energies in the environment. We are affected by sunlight and wind, the energy of the food we eat and the energy fields of other people. Even though we are not consciously aware of it, we are affected by the energy of colour. We are consciously aware of the colours we choose for our clothes or in our homes. Most of us notice colour some of the time and are aware of how we feel about certain colours.

This is especially highlighted in our dreams when a particular colour is prominent and we remember it. The clearer the colour, the more accurate the description of that symbol. The muddier the colour, the more that area is blocked or suppressed. *See* individual colours for their meaning.

Cooking Cooking in a dream tells the dreamer that it is possible that their ideas and plans can transform a situation.

Cripple If the dreamer is crippled, the dream is pointing out their fear of being incapacitated, helpless or powerless. What in the dreamer's life do they feel handicapped by? Perhaps the dream shows a need for help and support.

Crocodile The dreamer must examine their real feelings, which lie covered under their exterior.

Crossroad The dreamer has reached a turning point in their life. Where to go next is the dreamer's own choice. It is time for the dreamer to make a decision.

Crow The unconscious is trying to tell the dreamer to assess their personal integrity.

Dance Dancing is the prelude to lovemaking and is vital for relaxation, following the body's natural rhythm and self-expression. It puts the dreamer in touch with their animal behaviour and symbolises their joy.

Darkness This symbolises the dreamer's shadow side, the dark side of their personality – that which is hidden in their unconscious. Perhaps the dreamer feels 'in the dark' about something.

Daughter The dreamer's feminine aspect of their personality that connects them with their inner child is symbolised in this dream. If the dreamer has a daughter, then the link is probably with a facet of her personality.

Dead Body To dream of a dead body indicates that something of the dreamer's has been denied life, perhaps potential not being expressed, or love. It is possible the dreamer has talents they are not using or maybe they were not allowed to do something they really wanted to do as a child. A person who has been hurt emotionally by a love affair may have deadened their feelings towards members of that sex. In a dream, this dead part of the dreamer can be shown as a dead body.

Death Death can symbolise the ending of one particular way of being, making way for the birth of something new.

Deer The message of this dream is compassion, not just for others but for the self.

Desert The dreamer has feelings of desolation and emptiness, a void. They feel lost and alone. Can help or support be found anywhere?

Devil This is a symbol of the dreamer's shadow or dark side of their personality, representing their repressed anger and fear. The dream highlights the dreamer's inner conflict.

Digging Digging symbolises the hopeful search for 'treasure'. The dreamer should examine what that treasure is for them.

Dirt If something is dirty in a dream, it shows the dreamer's disappointment about something linked with whatever has dirt on it.

Diving The dreamer is being told by their unconscious to dive into their inner world and explore their emotions.

Divorce Whether or not divorce is relevant for the dreamer, divorce is a symbol of the separation that comes from conflict. It could be the fear of separation and loss, or a need for independence and autonomy.

Doctor The dreamer needs to be healed in some way or to be looked after.

Dog Dogs symbolise the dreamer's need to balance their sense of loyalty with their need for approval.

Dolphin This creature with its sense of humour and love of imitating human behaviour symbolises freedom of emotional expression. Perhaps it is time for the dreamer to express themself.

Donkey Either patience or stubbornness are the topic of dreams involving donkeys. How does the dreamer feel about being of service to others?

Door If the door is open and the dreamer wants to go through then the dreamer knows that soon there will be an opportunity of some kind for them. A closed door indicates feelings of rejection.

Dragon This represents life force and power. The dream suggests the dreamer needs to overcome fear.

Drowning Feelings of panic, of suffocation and of drowning indicate that the dreamer is being overwhelmed by their feelings.

Drum Is the beat of the drum repetitive or rhythmical? There is a message for the dreamer, perhaps they have not yet understood what it means to them.

Eagle This symbolises seeing things from a higher perspective, connecting with the higher mind.

Ear This indicates the need for the dreamer to listen carefully to what is being said to them by the unconscious in the dream.

Earthquake The dreamer's fear of being out of control and their feelings of powerlessness are shown in this dream. What is the upheaval about?

Eating To eat in dreams indicates a need for fulfilment and satisfaction in some area of the dreamer's life. Is the dreamer able to swallow and digest what is happening in the dream? Is the food what they want?

Egg This symbolises a need for wholeness in the dreamer's life. It can also symbolise new beginnings and growth.

Eight After seven, eight is symbolic of the death of the old and the beginning of the new. So the number eight occurring in a dream may indicate the start of something new for the dreamer.

Elephant This docile, thick-skinned and powerful animal symbolises something that needs to be remembered and the importance of being able to forgive and forget.

Elk To dream of elk implies the dreamer has a need for stamina. The dream may be suggesting that it would be helpful for the dreamer to seek out the company of their own gender for a while.

Excrement This is a symbol of the dreamer's feelings towards themself. The circumstances of the excrement in the dream will be an indication of how the unconscious sees the dreamer sabotaging things in their life.

Expedition To be involved in an expedition or to see a party of explorers in a dream is probably the unconscious urging the dreamer to take action and get more emotionally involved in their own personal adventures.

Eye Eyes are used in many ways in dreams. They represent the state of a relationship and they indicate what state the human psyche is in. Eyes sometimes show the dreamer's need for contact with someone. Avoiding eye contact or closed eyes in a dream indicates the dreamer has a fear of intimacy. Eyes can also represent how the dreamer sees their world.

———

Face Whatever type of face the dreamer sees in their dream reflects a facet of their personality. The dreamer may be concerned with their self-image and how they are seen by others. The face may play contradictory roles: hiding or expressing inner feelings. What face is the dreamer showing to the world and does it match how they feel inside?

Fairy The dreamer could use the images and messages in fairy stories to help them work out their own process in life. This dream could help connect the dreamer with their own childhood memories and fantasies.

Falling This reflects the dreamer's uncertainty about where they are in their life. The dream shows the dreamer is insecure and fearful of being out of control.

Family A dream about a family will reflect the dreamer's feelings about their own family – whether the dreamer is happy in that family or whether they want a different family. It symbolises love and rivalry, the struggle for individuality, but also a need for security in a warm, loving family. The dreamer needs to address their relationship with their mother and father and relevant members of their family.

Fat This could indicate a fear of becoming fat or becoming pregnant. The dreamer feels a need for protection. Depending on how the dreamer feels in the dream about being fat, a dream of this nature is telling them not to suppress their feelings.

Father This is the male archetype and the masculine aspect of the dreamer's personality. The father in the dream could represent a part of the dreamer or the dreamer's own father. How does the dreamer feel about their own father? Is the father in the dream a figure of authority and dominance, or a loving and supportive figure? Is he kind and gentle or cruel and abusive?

Fear This represents the dreamer's own fear. The fear, whatever it is about, needs to be addressed.

Feet These represent the dreamer's foundations, being grounded. In reflexology, the meridians for the body's organs are situated in the feet, so the feet are also responsible for supporting the body, and represent the fundamental issues in the dreamer's life. The dream may be saying to the dreamer, 'Stand on your own two feet,' or 'You've got your feet on the ground,' or 'You've put your foot in it this time.'

Fire The passionate and powerful feelings of the dreamer are symbolised in this dream – the bigger the fire, the more intense the feelings.

Fish Renewal and rebirth are symbolised by fish. This dream suggests that the dreamer has got in touch with something deep in their unconscious.

Five The number five symbolises the dreamer's life force. The human body has five fingers, five toes and five appendages. Thus dreaming of the number five is the unconscious highlighting something physical, something active and energetic – perhaps adventure and freedom. Because of this it can also point to change or uncertainty, curiosity and expansion. Five is the age for starting full-time education, the first time a child has to leave the family for any length of time.

Floating The significance depends on whether floating was a pleasant experience for the dreamer or one of feeling out of control. Floating is about being carried. Is the dreamer being carried along by something or being carried away? Is the floating on air or water?

Flood The dream is pointing to overwhelming emotions which engulf the dreamer. It could also indicate a need to sweep away old beliefs.

Flying The dreamer wishes to take flight from what is going on in their life. They have a wish to transcend and overcome difficulties and a desire for freedom. The dreamer wants to be higher, or more powerful, than something, or to see things from a more distant perspective.

Forest This symbolises a need for strength and protection in the dreamer's life. Metaphorically, 'seeing the wood for the trees' indicates a need for clarity. The depth and darkness of the forest can symbolise the unconscious and the shadow side of the dreamer.

Fountain Intuition and rejuvenation are symbolised by the fountain. The dreamer has a need for healing and should pay attention to the other details of the dream.

Four The number four symbolises wholeness, the integration of the four states of being: thinking, feeling, sensation and intuition. There are four parts to humans: the emotional, the sexual, the physical and the spiritual. The world is strongly influenced by the combination or balance of the four elements: fire, water, earth and air. There are four stages of growth: death, decay, gestation and rebirth. There are four seasons. Four is the number of people in the 'nuclear' family – and so can symbolise position and status within a family.

Fox The fox is a cunning creature in that it can blend into its surroundings and observe the actions of others unnoticed. This dream is about watching what others do, rather than what they say.

Frog Cleansing the soul is symbolised by frogs. The message for the dreamer is to give themself time to do whatever they need to feel refreshed.

Gambling Is it safe for the dreamer to take a chance on something? The rest of the dream will indicate how they feel. Perhaps it is time for the dreamer to take a risk.

Garden The details of the garden need to be considered. What is the state of the garden? The dreamer may need to pay attention to details and sort things out. It could also signify a need for peace and tranquillity or feelings of satisfaction.

Ghost This will symbolise someone very important to the dreamer. Perhaps the ghost is a reminder of unfinished business with that person.

Glass Depending on the other features and details of the dream, glass signifies fragility and a message to be careful.

Glove There is something the dreamer doesn't want to touch. Perhaps they have something to hide, or there is something in the dreamer's life that needs careful handling.

Goat Goats in dreams are the lusty side of the dreamer's personality, the sexuality that is hidden.

Gold Gold signifies a special quality in something. Perhaps something is turning into gold. The dreamer may be placing importance and value on that something.

Grandparent To dream of either grandparent relates to the dreamer's relationship with the particular grandparent. It also relates to the dreamer's relationship with parents and connections with childhood. The dreamer should focus on their history and background.

Grasshopper Perhaps the unconscious is asking whether the dreamer is wasting their time and energy on something.

Green The colour green symbolises the beginning of the healing process and stimulates the need to feel secure, certain, powerful and loved. Green is about peace and harmony, and deep feelings felt in the heart. It helps to calm the dreamer's feelings of doubt and insecurity.

Grouse Grouse symbolise the spiral – the way the dreamer's energy functions and connects with the things in their life, past and present.

Hair To dream about hair relates to the dreamer's feelings about themself and their appearance. Loss of hair shows insecurity and anxiety. Cutting hair shows a desire for something different. Plaiting hair indicates a desire for closeness and connectedness.

Hand Creativity, ideas, the things the dreamer holds on to, contact, touching and grasping can all be symbolised by hands. Hands in dreams highlight self-expression and the things the dreamer would really like to do. Alternatively, the unconscious may be telling the dreamer, 'You have the upper hand,' or 'Keep your hands off.'

Hawk The dreamer needs to be aware of the messages and signals that life is sending them and to look out for any hazards.

Head The brain, thoughts and ideas are all strongly symbolised in dreams by the head. If there are problems with the dreamer's head in a dream, the message is to stop worrying.

Heart Joy, happiness and excitement may be shown by dreaming of the heart, yet the heart may be heavy, symbolising sadness or self-pity.

Hedge Feelings of restriction, being blocked or stuck are symbolised by hedges. What does the dreamer need to do before they can go forward? Perhaps the dreamer is 'hedging their bets', trying to get away with not taking a risk.

Hole Holes represent the fear of the unknown, falling into something scary and feeling out of control. The message for the dreamer is that the hole represents something important. It could be something that is missing.

Holiday To dream of being on holiday symbolises the dreamer's wish to be in a different frame of mind or environment – to see things from a different perspective. There is a need for a time for fun and relaxation as a way of gaining strength.

Horse Dreaming of this magnificent animal is a reminder to the dreamer that their energy and power are at their disposal.

Hospital A need to be looked after and to be 'made better' is symbolised by hospitals. They can show the dreamer how to get in touch with their vulnerability. Dreams of hospitals can indicate the dreamer's fear of illness and being hospitalised, but mainly stand for a need to be healed.

Hotel This shows a need for anonymity and to be resting in a place of safety for a while.

House A house symbolises the dreamer as a whole, body and soul. Each room represents an undiscovered aspect of the unconscious and a different aspect of the dreamer's personality. The dreamer needs to pay attention to where they are in the house, what is happening and how they feel. How does the dreamer feel about each different room? Are some rooms easier to find or go into than others? The details will be of importance. Pay attention to everything: corridors, attics, cellars, windows, walls, doors, fireplaces, gardens etc.

Hummingbird If the dreamer feels trapped or imprisoned the joyful side of their personality could be suppressed. The dream's message is to relax, enjoy life and forget judgements.

Hunger This dream points out the dreamer's hunger for something – a need for nourishment, fulfilment and knowledge or a need for love, affection and security.

Hurricane The dreamer's overwhelming emotions are symbolised by the hurricane. It points out destruction, devastation and damage.

Hurt To feel physical pain in a dream indicates the dreamer's emotional hurts.

Ice This dream is saying that all the dreamer's feelings and emotions are frozen. Their heart is closed. The dream could also point to the dreamer's rigidity.

Iceberg/Icicle The dreamer should soon start to look at what is under the surface or at the tip of the iceberg. The dream shows a need for some kind of emotional release, perhaps the dreamer's tears need to start flowing.

Idol The dreamer has placed someone on a pedestal. This symbolises the dreamer's need for guidance and approval from someone else.

Illness Illness forces the body to rest. The dream could be saying that it is important for the dreamer to stop for a while. Nothing can be done at the moment. The dreamer should wait, then look at things with fresh energy.

Ink This symbolises that clearness and clarity are important for the dreamer to state their case or voice their opinion.

Invisibility The dreamer may be wondering whether it is safe to expose their vulnerability. Do they feel unnoticed or unheard?

Iron Strength, will power and determination are symbolised in this dream. Is it always necessary for the dreamer to be strong?

Island An island is the symbol of aloneness and isolation. Perhaps the dreamer is spending too much time alone. Maybe they need solitude in order to work something out.

Jam The jam could symbolise that the dreamer is in a jam or stuck, perhaps they feel frustrated. There could be a need for more sweetness in the dreamer's life.

Jealousy This reflects the dreamer's true feelings and fear of loss or separation. Insecurity, lack of self-esteem and feelings of worthlessness are indicated. The dreamer feels left out, and has a need for attention and love.

Jellyfish The feminine aspect of the dreamer's unconscious and/or something the dreamer feels squeamish about are symbolised by jellyfish.

Jewellery The dreamer needs to feel special and to enhance themself in some way. They have a need for attention and recognition, and to feel valued.

Joker The joker questions how serious the dreamer feels about something. Perhaps the dreamer wants to be taken more seriously. The joker can also be telling the dreamer to be more light-hearted and to honour their playfulness.

Journey This symbolises the dreamer's journey through life. Attention should be paid to the details of the journey. What is the mode of transport? Are they moving quickly or slowly? How far are they going? Where are they going? How does the dreamer feel?

Judge Is the dreamer being judged and by whom? Are they being judged fairly or unfairly? Is the dreamer being judgmental about something or someone? Does the dreamer worry too much about what other people think?

Juggler Is the dreamer trying to juggle too many things at once? This indicates the dreamer's struggle to stay in control.

Jump Is the dreamer ready to take a quantum leap into the unknown? The dreamer must examine what is making them jump and how this makes them feel. Perhaps the dreamer can find an alternative path rather than the dangerous leap.

Junk How does the dreamer feel about the junk in the dream? Is it the dreamer's junk or someone else's? Does the dreamer want to keep it or get rid of it? Is the dreamer overloaded with emotional baggage that they need to get rid of? The dream points out what is no longer needed in the dreamer's life. Perhaps these are old feelings, ideas and values.

Kangaroo Perhaps the dreamer is restless or has boundless energy.

Kennel This symbolises the 'dog house'. Does the dreamer feel in the dog house or do they want to put someone else there?

Kettle Is the dreamer waiting for the kettle to boil, waiting patiently or impatiently for something to happen? The kettle signifies the boiling or boiling over of the dreamer's emotions. Perhaps the

kettle has boiled dry and the dreamer feels empty.
Putting the kettle on can indicate a need for
stability, normality and comfort.

Key This tells the dreamer they have the key
within themself that will unlock and solve some
current difficulties. The message for the dreamer is
that problems will be overcome. The door to
whatever the dreamer wants can be opened.

Killing The dreamer may need to get rid of some
unwanted aspect of their own personality. Perhaps
it symbolises the killing off of old beliefs and
behaviours. To kill someone indicates the dreamer's
strong feelings toward that particular person and
the elimination of whatever the dreamer was
threatened by. Killing a parent indicates getting rid
of the way the dreamer has related to that
particular parent. Killing a child is about the
dreamer's killing of their own outmoded or
inappropriate behaviour. To dream of killing
indicates the dreamer has a need for empowerment
and growth.

Kiss A need for love and recognition and to feel
united with someone is strongly shown by
dreaming of kissing. Perhaps it is even a sign of
conquest. It can indicate the uniting of the
masculine and feminine within the dreamer.

Knife This symbolises the need to cut away what
is no longer needed in the dreamer's life. It can
also signify that which is sharp or cutting, perhaps
anger expressed in a covert way. A knife also
symbolises penetration – emotionally, physically or

sexually. Or it may show the dreamer's fear of being invaded in some way.

Knitting This is the connection of something important for the dreamer. The need to unify and heal, to mend or repair something is implied. The dreamer has a need to see the pattern in their life emerging, and to look at what has been created.

Labyrinth The dreamer is in a situation where they feel there is no way out.

Ladybird Ladybirds symbolise childhood and that some things are actually quite simple.

Lamb Is the dreamer allowing themself to be easily lead? Does the dreamer feel they are making unnecessary sacrifices in their life?

Lamp/Lantern This illuminates whatever the dreamer needs to see in their life. The quality of the light signifies that which is most conscious. It can be a welcoming relief for the dreamer to see the answer to something.

Land This symbolises the dreamer's need to feel grounded and secure.

Larder If the larder is full, it signifies that the dreamer has enough emotional resources and support. There is enough food for thought. If the larder is empty the dreamer has drained their resources and needs to put back some energy.

Laughter As in waking life, laughter is a release of tension, a reminder that life can be fun. The unconscious is telling the dreamer that they may be taking themself too seriously.

Laundry The need to start afresh or to look at things differently is symbolised by laundry. The dreamer may need to 'clean up their act'. Perhaps it shows a wish to get rid of their negative feelings.

Leech Being drained of energy in some way or taking advantage of someone or something are symbolised in dreams by leeches.

Leg The dreamer's motivation and support system are symbolised by legs. Their confidence and their ability to move and to run away are subjects that are highlighted in this dream. If the dreamer loses the use of their legs, or their legs are weakened, this signifies the dreamer's difficulties in carrying on with something in their life.

Letter This symbolises communication either directly or indirectly. The dreamer should write down their thoughts and feelings.

Library In a library there are plenty of books and information for the dreamer to choose from. What is the dreamer looking for? What do they want to find out? Dreaming of a library can also indicate the dreamer's hunger for knowledge and a need for the right atmosphere.

Lift The significance depends on whether the dreamer has a fear of lifts. It can symbolise the dreamer's fear of something going wrong. Possibly this is a fear of being stuck, trapped or out of control. It can also indicate the wish to rise above whatever is going on in the dreamer's life.

Lion A test of courage may or may not be needed. The dreamer should examine their anger and their power. Leadership and what that means for the dreamer are symbolised by lions.

Lizard To dream of a lizard is the unconscious attempting to say something about dreaming and meditation. Answers can be found if the dreamer looks inside themself.

Lose/Lost The dreamer's fear of losing something vital is being highlighted. There is realisation that something has been lost and has gone. Being lost indicates the dreamer's fear of not being able to cope. The dream also indicates being at a loss or being uncertain about the future.

Lynx The dreamer should listen to their intuition and pay attention to mental pictures or images. This dream is about the knowledge of secrets and the ability to see what is being hidden.

Machinery This symbolises the inner workings of the dreamer's unconscious, telling the dreamer that the wheels are in motion even if they are unaware.

Magician A magician in a dream symbolises empowerment. The dreamer is being told that they have the resources and the power within them to get what they want.

Magnet Someone or something is attracting the dreamer's attention, drawing them nearer.

Magpie To see magpies in a dream perhaps implies that the dreamer has become over-superstitious.

Map Symbolically, it is the plan of the dreamer's journey, indicating that the dreamer wants to know where they are going.

Marriage The dreamer desires to be united with someone. It shows the need for security and a wish to relax and settle down. The dream points out the dreamer's romantic feelings toward someone. This may be a union of opposites and the integration of the masculine and feminine within the dreamer. Marriage shows the dreamer's desire for celebration and to be the focus of attention.

Mask Who is wearing the mask? What is being covered up? A mask signifies the dreamer's façade, not wanting to show their real face.

Meadow Dreaming about meadows shows a need for rejuvenation of the spirit by getting in touch with nature. This may encompass childhood memories – feeling young and carefree. The feeling is like Spring, a time of new growth.

Meat The details need to be paid attention to because meat signifies the heart of the matter, the essence of the dream. The sensual side of the dreamer is highlighted. However, death can also be signified by this dream.

Medium This signifies a message to the dreamer from their unconscious. The medium can be another aspect of the dreamer's personality.

Menstruation The unconscious is reminding the dreamer of the change from childhood to womanhood. It also points out that everything has its cycle.

Mermaid This is the archetypal symbol of the feminine and the fabled creature of the sea. The alluring feminine woman with the tail of a fish symbolises the dreamer's fantasy of something they cannot have.

Microscope How is the dreamer looking at things? Are they reading too much into a situation?

Milk This can symbolise mothering, a need to be nurtured, but may also represent semen, the 'milk' which the male produces. The masculine, or male energy symbolises a need for power and strength, rather than a need to be protected.

Mirror The mirror highlights the dreamer's persona, the protective mask they present to the world. It has two purposes, first to make a specific impression on other people, and second, to conceal the dreamer's inner self. The unconscious produces a mirror to highlight the difference between what the dreamer shows to the outside and what is felt by the dreamer on the inside.

Money Money signifies anything of equivalent value to the dreamer. This could be love, time, energy or self-esteem. A certain amount of money symbolises a certain length of time for something, so many days. Being short of money draws the dreamer's attention to the anxiety of being hard up and consequently not being able to meet current demands. It also symbolises lack of self worth. If something is expensive, the message for the dreamer is that perhaps the cost of something is too great. They will have to pay for what they do. Is it worth the cost?

Monster The dreamer's fear of something life threatening, the quest for immortality and the fear of their own death are all symbolised by monsters. The monster is an image of the dreamer's fear, perhaps the fear of the unknown. Which part of the dreamer does the monster represent? If the dreamer is being victimised by a ferocious monster, it would help them to go back into the dream in their imagination and fight it.

Moon To see the moon in a dream is the subconscious telling the dreamer to pay attention to their intuition. The moon represents the unconscious and the feminine aspect, implying a need for a time for inner reflection.

Moose Self-esteem is the subject of this dream. Has the dreamer given themself a pat on the back recently? They may need to.

Mother The feminine aspect reflects the part of the dreamer that their mother represents. This dream is highlighting the dreamer's relationship with their mother. The dream can indicate a need for comfort and nurturing.

Mountain The mountain indicates opportunities or obstacles in the dreamer's life. Progression towards a goal, also symbolising the climb or the struggle to the peak.

Mouse These animals symbolise paying attention to detail, to scrutinise, or to put everything in order. The dreamer needs to look at themself and others more carefully.

Mouth The mouth and the tongue are symbols of sexual and sensual pleasure, hunger and thirst. Consequently, the dreamer should examine the manner in which they express their needs and feelings. The unconscious may be chewing over some problem in the dream, or telling the dreamer to hold their tongue.

Mud Whatever is currently happening for the dreamer, mud indicates feeling stuck or held back, not being able to move forward yet. The mud symbolises being bogged down by something.

Muscle The muscles are a symbol of strength, confidence, being adequate and capable. They show the dreamer what is forceful, strong and powerful. Perhaps the dreamer has a desire for physical strength.

Naked How does the dreamer feel about being naked and defenceless? A dream of this nature can indicate feeling exposed or vulnerable or a need for the dreamer to drop their façade and stop pretending, thereby revealing the truth.

Narrow The dreamer is feeling restricted and being reminded of their limitations. There is no choice but to carry on until things become easier.

Neck The head and the body are connected by the neck, so consequently it symbolises in dreams the connection from feelings and sexuality to thinking and doing. Perhaps the dreamer sticking their neck out, or up to their neck in something.

Net The significance depends on how the dreamer felt about the net in the dream. Was it a safety net or a trap? Who or what does the dreamer want to capture in a net? Or, who wants to capture the dreamer? Or, why does the dreamer feel a need for a safety net? Is there a need to be rescued?

Nine Nine is the number prior to wholeness and perfection. Its significance lies in its strength. It is the highest single digit. There are nine months of pregnancy, it takes nine months of gestation for something to grow and develop, for something to be ready.

Nose The dreamer's curiosity and intuition are often symbolised in dreams by the nose.

Number In waking life numbers are relevant and important to us. People remember significant things in terms of counting and numbers: money, time, dates, people, things etc. In dreams the unconscious reminds the dreamer of this but quite often juggles them around in such a fashion that they become interchangeable.

Sometimes a dream contains a certain number of identical objects, the repeating of an event or something that has occurred often. This is the unconscious repeating something for the dreamer so that they will take notice of it.

It is important to understand this to try to make connections about the relevance of a specific number and what it means.

The dreamer will know which numbers hold special meaning for them, the others they will have to explore further. It is up to the dreamer to work out what their unconscious is telling them – for example £15 could be 15 years or 15 minutes. Or perhaps the dreamer was 15-years-old when something important happened. Odd numbers represent the masculine aspect, even the word 'odd' may be relevant. Even numbers represent the feminine aspect.

Numbers above ten with two or more digits can be added together to make a single number. For example 867 becomes 8+6+7 = 21. And applying the same operation again, 2+1 = 3.

It is up to the dreamer to work out the sequence of numbers in a dream and what they mean for them. If a number appears in a dream, it is an important clue to what it connects with in the dreamer's life. *See* individual numbers for their meaning.

Nun Nuns symbolise the dreamer's desire to connect with the spiritual side of their personality.

Nut Something in the dreamer's life may be 'hard to crack'. This dream can symbolise new life, potential yet to unfold or the gathering or saving of something for future use.

Oak The dreamer has a need for solidness, strength, groundedness and protection.

Oar An oar is something to hold on to within the sea of emotional imbalance. The dreamer wants to feel in control.

Oasis To dream of an oasis is the unconscious telling the dreamer that they need to find refuge and nourishment.

Ocean This symbolises the emotions and the unconscious. It show the depth of the dreamer's feelings about something. A rough sea with huge waves is telling the dreamer that they are feeling overwhelmed by their feelings.

Octopus An octopus in a dream symbolises the possessive and clinging mother.

One The number one symbolises independence, loneliness, aloneness and individuality. The dreamer is Number one. It shows unity or oneness with life. New beginnings and growth may be what the unconscious is hinting at. It could also symbolise the dreamer's desire to be alone – their fear of intimacy with another. Does the dreamer want to be an only child?

Orange The colour orange symbolises the need to find acceptance and reality through other people. It is a happy sociable colour: warm, hospitable, humanitarian, expansive and optimistic. Ambitious and competitive, orange in a dream points out to the dreamer that we are all the same really.

Orchestra The dreamer has a desire for harmony and synchronicity. Perhaps the dreamer needs to listen only to their own inner orchestra.

Orgasm Orgasm is a symbol of the dreamer's need for sexual fulfilment.

Ostrich Because of the ostrich's habit of sticking its head in the sand at any sign of trouble, it normally symbolises avoidance.

Otter The feminine within the dreamer and also the child are symbolised. The dream's message is to stop worrying and remember how to play.

Oven The oven symbolises incubation of an idea or a project that the dreamer wishes to create.

Owl Surprisingly, deception, as well as inner wisdom, can be the topic of a dream about owls.

Package If the dreamer sends a package in a dream, this indicates the letting go or return of something. To receive a package is the unconscious recognising a part of the dreamer which has not yet been acknowledged.

Pain Even if this is a physical pain, it is indicating to the dreamer that they are hurting emotionally. There is an emotional wound that the dreamer needs to address.

Paint Painting in dreams is the creating of something or the covering up of something no longer important. It shows the desire to start afresh. *See also* Colour.

Palace The dreamer desires to be surrounded by affluence and magnificence and to feel good about their life and themself.

Panda This dream highlights the dreamer's need for comfort and security.

Parrot The parrot is a dream symbol for copying, imitating, repetition and insincerity.

Passport The passport is a symbol of identity. It could be a way for the unconscious to say, 'This is who I am'.

Pelvis This part of the body represents sexuality and sensuality. It show how the dreamer feels about giving of themself and making connections or bonds with others. The dreamer should examine their feelings about reproduction and the sex act.

Pen/Pencil This indicates the dreamer's need to express themself and to communicate. It may be important to get something written down.

Penis This is a symbol of life's active, creative and vital force. The relationship the male dreamer has with his penis and the sex act is highlighted in this dream. It may point out how his fears, hurts and attitudes are influencing his sexual energy. For a woman to dream of a penis says something about her relationship with her own masculinity, her ambitions, her intellect and her aggression.

Perfume To smell perfume in a dream is the unconscious trying to remind the dreamer of an important memory. What emotions are evoked by the smell of perfume?

Pig The pig will symbolise that which is ugly and greedy in the dreamer's life.

Poison Anything which poisons or pollutes causes injury, illness or death. Does the dreamer feel something is poisoning them in some way? Perhaps the dreamer is poisoning themself with something. This can be an attitude, a relationship or a habit. They may want to get rid of someone or something unwanted in their life.

Police These people, being in a position of authority, signify rules, law and order. Seeing the police in a dream indicates that the dreamer may need help in getting their own life in order. Perhaps it points to the conflict between the dreamer's own conscience and conventional

morality and authority. The dreamer may have a
fear of being found out about something, or a fear
of being punished.

Porcupine This shows a need for the dreamer to
remember the things that brought them joy as a
child: innocence, fantasy and imagination. They
should remember that fear kills trust.

Pregnant This is a sign of potential new life.
Hopes and dreams seem positive and possible. The
dreamer may be about to give birth to a new idea
or emotion, or going in a new direction. Dreams of
pregnancy can also indicate the dreamer's desire to
be pregnant and have a child.

Prison The dreamer may feel imprisoned by
something in their waking life. They may be
creating their own rules which restrict them in
some way. One part of the dreamer's personality
may be restricting another part. They may have
unconsciously created rules about their own
behaviour which are confining them. The dreamer
may be punishing themself, or they may be trying
to keep their impulses under control.

Prostitute Dreaming of prostitutes signifies that
the dreamer is using energy inappropriately and
wasting their creativity. How much does the
dreamer value themself if they either have to pay
to get their needs met or sells themself to others in
order to meet other people's needs.

Puppet Manipulation is often symbolised in
dreams by a puppet. Who is being manipulated

here? It may be a reminder to the dreamer not to give their power away.

Purple The colour purple symbolises the dreamer's need to have relationships that are free from any conflict. It also points to a need to live life through the intuition, seeing beyond the complexities of what is really there. Purple is the colour of psychic awareness, the ability to tune into the inner world of other people.

Pyramid This symbolises any triangular relationship connected to the dreamer. Also it can symbolise being in the safe haven of the womb. It often represents a tomb or temple and connects the dreamer with their higher self.

Quarrel Sometimes issues that are unresolved in waking life can be resolved in a dream. To dream of quarrelling with someone highlights the dreamer's unexpressed anger or inner conflict.

Quay The dreamer could be unconsciously thinking of leaving something behind.

Queen The dreamer may be seeking approval from a regal and powerful woman. The dreamer could need to be recognised and to feel important. A queen often represents the dreamer's own mother.

Queue The dreamer feels that they have to wait their turn for something. They are waiting for some attention in order to get their needs met.

Quilt This is a sign of the dreamer's need for protection. If it is a patchwork quilt, the many different aspects of the dreamer's personality will come together to make a whole.

———

Rabbit The unconscious is reminding the dreamer that their fears can actually produce that which they fear most. The message to the dreamer is: stop worrying about things.

Race This is the symbol of competition, wanting to win and wanting to be there first. It shows the dreamer's struggle against time and the frustration of having to wait for something. Rivalry and the pace of life are also indicated.

Rain The cleansing process, the necessity for tears to flow and refresh the spirit are symbolised by dreaming of rain.

Rainbow The dreamer's need for reward after hard work is shown by this symbol, indicating that the unconscious feels that completion and celebration are not far away.

Rape This symbol shows feelings of invasion and penetration and the dreamer's fears of being forced to do something against their will. Perhaps the dreamer is feeling victimised and powerless.

Rat The rat symbolises the dreamer's fear or mistrust of a person or situation. It also represents their fear of disease or infestation.

Raven The raven symbolises magic, in that changes of consciousness or feelings do happen without a specific reason.

Red Red stimulates assertiveness and direct action. It is associated with sexual energy, physical excitement, anger, aggression, physical strength and danger. The colour red is telling the dreamer to do something now, that they do have the energy or motivation to accomplish their goals.

Repair The dreamer has a desire to put something right. It could be a relationship with someone or something within the dreamer's emotional life that needs to be healed.

Restaurant The significance of dreaming of restaurants depends on what restaurants mean for the dreamer, what memories they have. Eating out is about nourishment, being waited on, being looked after and so it may be the unconscious expressing a need for these things. Perhaps the dreamer is eating different food, implying that they want to try something different in life.

Riding Dreaming of riding symbolises the erotic side of the dreamer's personality and sexual attachment to someone. It shows the dreamer's need to feel powerful and in control of their life.

Ring The symbol of love and friendship can point to the dreamer's need for security.

River The flow of the dreamer's life is being shown. The significance depends on the state of the river in the dream. Is it fast or slow flowing? Is the dreamer immersed in the water or on the bank watching? Does they want to cross the river? Is there a bridge?

Road To dream of roads is the unconscious telling the dreamer something about their direction in life. All details need to be paid attention to. Is the road straight or winding, smooth or rocky, wide or narrow? Are there forks or crossroads, turnings, dead-ends? Is it uphill or downhill? Whatever the details, they represent the dreamer's life or struggle at the time, and where they feel their life is going. Where does the dreamer want it to go?

Robin This dream suggests the dreamer feels they deserve a slice of good luck.

Rock Rocks symbolise feeling alone and isolated. They show a need for stability, security, safety and groundedness. They are linked with the archetypal mother figure.

Room A room represents a hidden part of the unconscious. The details of the room are of importance. What is in the room? What does it feel like? Is there a particular room the dreamer doesn't want to be in?

Rope The umbilical cord and the attachment to mother are represented by rope. The dreamer is attached to something or someone. Perhaps the dreamer yearns for something to hold on to. They may want help and need to be rescued. Alternatively, they feel tied up and restricted.

Running Running away indicates the dreamer's fear of facing something. It could be a situation they are not ready for, or something they are deeply afraid of. Depending on the emotions felt in the dream, running also indicates a wish for events to happen quickly, racing toward a particular goal.

Rust Whatever the object, or connection with the rusty object, the message for the dreamer is that something isn't being used to its full potential and is wasting away.

Sacrifice Any kind of sacrifice in a dream is telling the dreamer that perhaps they are being a martyr, or doing something they don't want to do. The message here is that there is a choice and that the dreamer is in control of their own life.

Sand This symbolises illusion. Is the dreamer seeing things differently from how they really are? Perhaps something in the dreamer's life is less solid than it appears. The unconscious is telling them that nothing is permanent and that things change.

Saw Creating something or cutting something down to size is symbolised by dreaming of a saw. The dreamer may be cutting away what is not wanted, or shaping up their plans.

Scar This is a reminder to the dreamer of a past emotional wound which, even though it has healed, is still remembered. What is its purpose in the dreamer's life now?

School School is the earliest experience of social convention and has huge emotional impact on a child. Consequently it is well remembered by the unconscious. School is used in dreams to show up the dreamer's current conflict. Whatever the incident in school was, it will still be relevant in the dreamer's life today.

Searching The dreamer is likely to know what they are looking for, but perhaps finding it may involve difficult consequences or implications.

Season The human psyche is deeply affected by the changing seasons. In a dream each season will represent an important part of who the dreamer is. When we were born, when our siblings were born, term times, holiday times, anniversaries of births and deaths are relevant to how we feel about the changing seasons. There are monthly cycles, yearly cycles, cycles of growth, death and rebirth.

Dreaming also follows these cycles of nature throughout the year. We all have our personal feelings and memories relevant to each season. If the dreamer dreams about a particular season it is important to look at what happened in their life at that particular time of year. *See* individual seasons for their meaning.

Seed Seeds signify the dreamer's need to start again, the wish for a new chance.

Seesaw Who is on the seesaw with the dreamer? The seesaw symbolises a power struggle that is going up and down but is not being resolved.

Selling Who is the dreamer trying to convince about something, themself or someone else? This indicates the selling of an idea to someone else for the dreamer's benefit, or something the dreamer wants to get rid of to someone else.

Seven Seven is known as the number of wisdom. Traditionally, the seventh day is devoted to God. There are seven virtues, vices and deadly sins. In astrology there are seven-year cycles of growth. At the age of seven, the child has also completed a cycle of growth, so there is a sense of completion around the number seven.

Shadow The unconscious, the shadow side of the dreamer's personality which is normally hidden or unknown is symbolised by shadow.

Shark The fear of hidden dangers is symbolised by the shark; perhaps also the misuse of power.

Sheep Whoever is being represented by the sheep is being taken advantage of, following without using their judgement – trusting without thinking.

Shell If the dreamer dreams of a shell, it can signify emptiness. Perhaps the dreamer feels there is nothing there for them any more. Or the dreamer may have gone into their shell, closing themself off from the outer world. The shell may also imply that the dreamer requires a time of non-activity, protection, and of waiting before growth.

Ship A ship could be the vessel used for the dreamer's journey through their emotional life. The

circumstances of the journey need to examined.
The vessel represents the 'self', the dreamer as a
whole. Going off to sea symbolises independence,
making a break from the family.

Shooting To dream of shooting symbolises hopes
and ambitions. The dreamer is focusing energy on
a particular goal and wants to win.

Shopping Shopping indicates that there are many
choices available to the dreamer. But does the
dreamer have the resources to buy what they want?
The dreamer does however have a decision to
make about something in their life.

Shoulder The ability to bear or to carry the
responsibilities of what life brings rest on the
dreamer's shoulders. They will indicate the
dreamer's load and also signify the need for support
from someone else. The unconscious could be
telling the dreamer that they have a chip on their
shoulder, or that they need a shoulder to cry on.

Silk A desire for an easier life in terms of riches
and luxury is symbolised. So are sensuality and the
desire for eroticism.

Singing The dreamer often experiences joy in a
dream where they are singing. Singing indicates
that the dreamer has a voice and they are using it
to its fullest.

Sister Often a sister can be symbolic of feminine
support, nurturing and friendship. However, a sister
can also symbolise rivalry and jealousy.

Six Six is the number of harmony, equilibrium and balance. A six-pointed star is formed out of two triangles, one points up and the other points down. This symbolises the balance between heaven and earth. The number six is the multiplication of three, the masculine number, and two, the feminine number, equalling six or sex. Six also is the number relating to the evolution of life. Is the number six relevant to the number of people in the dreamer's family?

Skeleton To dream of a skeleton indicates the dreamer's need to get to the bare bones of a problem. It can also symbolise emptiness in the dreamer's life. After death and decay there is nothing left but bones. Is there something in the dreamer's life that remains unacknowledged?

Skin This symbolises the dreamer's persona, their external covering. What kind of skin is it? What kind of façade or exterior is the dreamer presenting to the world?

Skunk The ability to attract or repel others is symbolised by the skunk. The dreamer needs to be aware of the people they are attracted to and who are attracted to them. They must also be careful of leaking sexual energy or playing games. What kind of energy is the dreamer emitting in their life at the moment?

Sleeping To dream of being asleep indicates that some aspect of the dreamer's personality is asleep, hidden away. Perhaps it is time to awaken that which has been shut away.

Smoke Smoke in a dream tells the dreamer that there is fire somewhere. It suggests that there is unexpressed anger that could explode at any time.

Snail Are things moving too slowly or does the dreamer need to slow down?

Snake The snake symbolises transmutation, the ability to keep changing from one form to another. For the dreamer it represents the necessity to grow and change, and to survive the struggle that goes with that change.

Soldier Does the dreamer want someone to do their fighting for them, a hero figure? This dream may symbolise some conflict going on within the dreamer or could show the dreamer's need for organisation and discipline.

Spider The dreamer must find new ways to solve a current problem. Perhaps things have become too complicated, so that the dreamer doesn't notice that there are alternative solutions.

Sponge Dreaming of a sponge indicates a soaking up of energy, either the dreamer's or someone else's.

Spring Springtime is a time for new direction, renewed energy and growth. The dreams that occur during the spring deal with issues concerning childhood, motherhood and open contact with others. Dreaming of the spring indicates the desire to start again with fresh energy and optimism. It shows the dreamer wants to make changes, to have fun, to be happy and to be relieved of difficulties.

Spy The dreamer is not feeling safe. They may feel watched. They have a fear of intrusion and invasion. The dream could indicate that, in their involvement with another person, the dreamer is neglecting their own interests.

Squirrel The importance of gathering and storing energy for further need and reserving something for further use is demonstrated by the squirrel. It could be that the dreamer has too many things they don't need. They may have to let something go.

Stairs A staircase indicates the possibility of climbing to another level so the dreamer can have a look and see what is upstairs. The dream may show a desire for a higher level of material success, to rise above what is going on in life now or to look at things from a different perspective. Perhaps the dreamer is too emotionally involved and would benefit from being more detached.

Star This is a symbol of a birth. The dream shows the dreamer's desire for success and recognition, for guidance and insight, and the divine truth.

Statue This stationary figure shows that the dreamer's feelings and emotions are frozen, stuck. Emotionally, the dreamer feels immobile, lifeless. Their energy and strength are paralysed. Some aspect of the dreamer's personality may have died.

Stomach The dreamer's natural drives, hunger and digestion, both physical and psychological, are represented by the stomach. Is there something in the dreamer's life that they cannot stomach, or something painful that gives them belly ache? We hold a great deal of our emotions in the stomach, so to dream of the stomach indicates the need to see which feelings are being held in there.

Stone What was once a living experience is now a dead memory. Stones could indicate the dreamer's difficulties in relating emotionally with others. Perhaps the dreamer is afraid to express how they really feel and to be seen to be vulnerable. They may feel hurt by the stony reaction of others. Being hit with stones indicates being punished.

Storm Storms are the dreamer's outbursts of emotion, desire or energy. They show extreme mental agitation, thinking and worrying. Violent passions and explosive feelings are symbolised. They point to the dreamer's fear of what might happen if feelings are expressed.

Sucking These show the dreamer's concern over the draining of resources, of being sucked dry. Alternatively, they symbolise the sucking up of new ideas, nourishment and new energy, the dreamer's need for sustenance.

Suicide The dreamer's desire to kill off aspects of themselves is symbolised. Their need to give up is shown. Self-punishment and self-persecution are the subjects of this dream, signifying a deep-seated unhappiness. A great deal depends on how the dreamer feels about their own suicide.

Summer Summertime is about richness and abundance, freedom of spirit. Dreams during the summertime are often about thought processes, inventions and new ideas. To dream of the summer symbolises youth, life at its most fruitful, the blossoming of love and the fulfilment of the energy started in the spring. The dreamer wishes for fun, laughter and relaxation. They want to be carefree and frivolous.

Sun This represents the light of consciousness, the intellect. It suggests the advent of new realisations about something, hope and potential progress.

Swan This magnificent white bird is a symbol of healing and transformation. It symbolises change and different states of consciousness. The swan's message for the dreamer is to relax and allow the transformation to occur. The dreamer should go with the flow, while paying attention to intuition.

Sweets Sweets symbolise small rewards, tokens of affection. They can also symbolise a token of apology for the withholding of affection and love.

Swimming The emotional effort the dreamer is putting into their life is symbolised by swimming. Is it easy for the dreamer to stay afloat or are they swimming against the current?

Sword A sword symbolises the dreamer's defence, and also their ability to cut through their problems. The dreamer is reacting in a ruthless and practical way, using intellect rather than emotions.

Syrup The dreamer being over-emotional and sentimental is being symbolised. The dream is saying that something is too sweet and sickly to be sincere. Alternatively, the dream may point to a sticky situation in the dreamer's life.

Tap To hear a tapping noise in a dream indicates the unconscious is trying to draw the dreamer's attention to something.

Teacher Teachers represent the dreamer's concept of authority. However, the teacher may be the part of the unconscious that teaches the dreamer. What lessons need to be learned?

Tear This highlights the dreamer's sadness about something and allows the dreamer to examine their feelings of loss or unhappiness.

Teeth Dreaming of teeth symbolises biting into a problem, chewing over something. An infected tooth signifies decay and the need to get to the root of a problem. Teeth falling out symbolise growing up, moving on to a new phase. Also this can show a fear of losing face or something spoiling the dreamer's appearance. The loss of the dreamer's teeth shows the fear of losing something important or a loss of power.

Telephone The telephone symbolises the dreamer's need for contact, getting in touch. The dream may be telling them to make contact with their unconscious, and listen to what the dream is telling them. It might show a need to be heard and a need for physical contact.

Ten Ten signifies wholeness and perfection which comes from completion. A numerical cycle is completed, so ten is ready to return to one again. The number ten can signify happiness and bliss, or struggle and sorrow. Everything is encompassed in the number ten. Ten can be one, zero or ten.

Theatre A theatre represents the dreamer's mind, the action of the play and what is happening. Thoughts and images are acted out through the dreamer's own internal dialogue.

Threat Threatening words often represent the dreamer's own conscience and their own voice. The words could be telling the dreamer what they already know and don't want to hear, or something they are refusing to understand.

Three The number three is symbolic of triangular relationships, such as the mother, father and child relationship and the male genitals. Because of the inherent unevenness of three – two and one or one and two – there is the possibility of one being left out. Can there be equal harmony with three? The number three can relate to the three states of being: parent, adult and child. The dreamer relates to others in only one of these groups at a time.

Thunder This indicates the dreamer's hostility or rage. It shows a need in the dreamer to release their suppressed feelings.

Tidal Wave These are overwhelming feelings that the dreamer feels will engulf them, highlighting their fear of upheaval.

Tightrope The dreamer's intense need for survival and their fear of falling from grace is very strongly signified by dreaming of being on a tightrope. This shows just how stressed and under pressure the dreamer is feeling.

Toilet Dreaming of toilets highlights and connects the dreamer with their basic bodily requirements and how they feel about themself. They need to purge unwanted memories and bad experiences.

Tomb The dreamer's feelings of restriction and immobilisation are highlighted by this dream. The dreamer will know how to break free, they just need to be brave and take a risk.

Tongue *See* Mouth.

Toy This connects the dreamer with memories of their childhood, how they played then. Is the dreamer able to play now? Do they allow themself to play and have fun?

Train The train represents the dreamer's vitality and passions, their individual progress on their journey and their trains of thought. Missing the train indicates fear of missing an opportunity or not making the progress they had hoped for. How does the dreamer feel about getting off the train, arriving at their destination?

Tunnel This symbolises the passageway to the self, the connection between the conscious and the unconscious. It relates to the experience of being born and may point to a regressive desire to withdraw from the outside world, to go back into the womb and then emerge afresh, making new contact with the outside world.

Turkey The dreamer should examine how much of themselves they are giving to others and what are their motives for giving.

Turtle The dreamer's need for protection and how to use it is represented by the turtle. It may be time for the dreamer to take their feelings seriously and to attack if necessary.

Twins Twins represent two sides of the same person: the dreamer. They point out to the dreamer that there are two sides to a problem or situation in the dreamer's life.

Two The number two can symbolise duality, a couple, two halves of anything, the masculine and the feminine, the balance of yin and yang or a pair. It can point to the need for another or can signify the comparison of two objects, an either/or situation. This may be an inner split, a conflict or polarities such as light and dark etc. Anything that comes in twos can be symbolised by this dream. The dream could say something about the second child in a family.

Tyre The dreamer may have a need for safety and groundedness, while being able to be mobile. A flat tyre indicates that the dreamer's energy is very low or out of balance.

Ulcer This may be the dreamer's inner frustration, their inability to express their anger fully or even at all. The dreamer is at war with themself – the ulcers are the result.

Umbrella The umbrella shows the dreamer's desire for shelter from the storms in their life.

Underground This represents the dreamer's unconscious. Was the dreamer able to see what is happening down there? How does it feel? All of the details will be relevant in some way. New growth cannot occur without first experiencing the pain of life underground.

Undertaker The dreamer believes that something that has to be undertaken is not going to be pleasant. Perhaps the dreamer has come to the end of a particular phase in their life and has to say goodbye to something or someone.

Undressed This is a symbol of the dreamer's fear of personal secrets being revealed and feeling the need to cover them up.

Unicorn The unicorn symbolises the union of opposites, the vitality and energy that occurs when conflict is resolved.

Uniform If the dreamer is wearing a uniform in their dream, this indicates their need to be the same as other people. It also symbolises authority and inflexibility – the need for respect. The dream can also point to sexual and erotic fantasies involving uniform.

University A university symbolises the place of learning within the dreamer, their desire to study and to gain knowledge. Perhaps the dream shows the dreamer is feeling the need to belong.

Upside-down Turning a situation upside-down, upheaval and change are necessary for the dreamer to see things from all aspects. The dreamer needs to find what they are looking for.

Urine In dreams urine symbolises sexual feelings or sexual energy.

Vacuum This indicates the dreamer is feeling stuck, trapped and isolated. The dreamer needs to escape in order to be creative again and for the energy to flow.

Vagina The hidden aspect of the female energy within the dreamer is often represented by the vagina. The dreamer may desire to be accepted or received within a female environment. In dreams the vagina symbolises the foundations, feelings and drives of the feminine: the ability to procreate and nurture, the wholeness of female sexuality, the sexual need and the desire for children. For a man to dream of a vagina suggests he has fears of meeting a woman's full sexuality and highlights the depth of his relationship with his mother.

Vampire The dreamer is in some way being exhausted and drained of their energy or vitality. They are allowing someone else to suck them dry.

Veil There is something that the dreamer wishes to keep partially covered about themself. Or there is something about the dreamer that they will only partially recognise. The dreamer will have to do the unveiling themself when they are ready.

Venereal Disease Dreaming of venereal diseases points to some relationship in the dreamer's life being diseased or incestuous. The unconscious is pointing out to the dreamer that something unhealthy is going on.

Vine Potential growth and fertility are symbolised by the vine. The dreamer is seeing things from a spiritual, rather than a practical perspective.

Virgin Whatever it is in the dream that is virginal, the message for the dreamer is a need for wholeness and purity within some aspect of their life. The Virgin Mary is symbolic of the female aspect of the religious part of the dreamer.

Voice It is important to listen to the message from any voice in a dream, even though it is likely to be the dreamer who is really doing the talking.

Vomit This is symbolic of the need to get rid of something very unwanted in the dreamer's life, something unpleasant and potentially harmful to the dreamer. The vomit also highlights a need to get rid of old beliefs and attitudes, to express what has been held back and get things out in the open.

Waiter This is the male aspect of the dreamer's personality, the part that gives to others. It is the side of the dreamer that needs to be of service to others in order to feel appreciated. To dream of being waited on might also show the other side of the coin – the desire to be served, nourished and looked after.

Walking The dreamer is making progress through their life at their own speed. Walking away from something or someone indicates the dreamer's desire to move on.

Wall Walls are symbolic of obstacles or blockages. The dreamer has created their own wall in their dream. What does the wall represent? What is it shutting out? Why has the dreamer created their own obstacle?

Wallet The dreamer's personal and private beliefs, thoughts and feelings are represented by the wallet. It is the private place for the dreamer's secrets.

Wand A magic wand symbolises that the dreamer is in control of their life and capable of achieving whatever they desire.

War This is probably a reflection of the dreamer's own inner conflict.

Washing This symbolises that the dreamer needs to wash away the past, make clean, forgive and start again. Or perhaps the dream is telling the dreamer that they need to give up on something or someone – to wash them away.

Wasp This dream signifies that the dreamer is feeling threatened by something.

Waste To see waste or waste land in a dream symbolises the dreamer's conflict between the creative and destructive sides of their personality.

Watch Depending on what a particular watch means for the dreamer, a watch usually symbolises that time is moving on.

Water Water is a symbol for many things. Because of water's connection with uterine fluid in the womb, it is sometimes a symbol for emerging life. Spiritual rebirth is also symbolised because of water's use in baptism. It may represent the fluid side of the dreamer's nature – their emotions and their deepest feelings. Tears, grieving and sadness are all shown by dreaming of water. Water is also the symbol of the feminine: of the unconscious, of womanhood and of the mother. The dreamer may need to renew their energy from the life force, to be immersed in water, to be reborn. The dreamer will know what their dream is telling them.

Wax The dreamer is associating the pliable wax with a situation or a feeling that can be remoulded or easily changed.

Wealth To dream of being wealthy indicates that the wisdom and experience within the dreamer is easily accessible.

Weather Weather usually signifies the health and emotional state of the dreamer. Clear and sunny weather indicate that the dreamer's balance of health is good. Cloudy, windy and stormy weather signify a lack of clarity and emotional turbulence. Grey skies signify flatness and a lack of energy.

Web The dreamer may be feeling trapped in some way within their home or domestic life. They may feel bound by their own anxiety.

Weed To dream of weeds is an indication to the dreamer that they are allowing themself to be overpowered by something in their life which is restricting their growth.

Weight The balance of justice, the conscience, is often symbolised by weight in dreams. If something appears to be heavy in a dream, it is making its presence felt. So, the more it weighs, the more important it is.

Whale The whale represents the dreamer's need to find their own voice and make the sounds they have to make to release tension or emotion.

Wheel Dreams which involve wheels will be important. The wheel could be the wheel of life, karma or destiny. The circular wheel indicates the continuation of life, death, decay, gestation and rebirth. It points to beginnings, endings, reaping, sowing and finally completion. Everything in life has a cycle.

Whisper The dreamer is finding it difficult to say what is in their heart. They are feeling held back or restricted by something.

White White is the colour that absorbs all other colours and dilutes them. It symbolises purity and innocence. Within a dream white relates to the dreamer's imagination and divine realisation. The colour white symbolises anything possessing the energy to transform feelings of negativity and restriction into feelings of positivity and freedom.

Window To dream of a window indicates to the dreamer that they do have eyes and that to look at something or to look out for something could be extremely helpful. The dreamer should examine their outlook on the world. How does the dreamer interpret the view from the window?

Winter Wintertime is the time of the year for hibernation and rest. It is the time of inner growth and going within. Dreams during the winter months are likely to concern the dreamer's spiritual awareness and deeply relate to the dreamer's past experiences. Dreaming of winter symbolises the dreamer's feelings of aloneness, feeling punished, left out in the cold, death and old age. The message for the dreamer is to see things as they really are. They must complete any grieving that needs to be done.

Witch The mother is represented by the witch. However, it is the negative aspect of mother, as in good or evil. It also shows the dark side of the female aspect of the dreamer, the embodiment of all that is nasty, fearsome or ugly. The dreamer may be worried about the loss of youth, becoming an old woman. Strangely, the witch can represent the wisdom within the dreamer as well.

Wolf The teacher within the dreamer is represented by the wolf. The dream is telling the dreamer to get in touch with their true self.

Womb This is a place of nourishment, safety and protection. It symbolises a place to rest and to gather strength for the dreamer.

Wrong To dream of doing something wrong, or being in the wrong place signifies that somewhere within the dreamer's life they have actually done something they feel to be wrong.

X-Ray This highlights the dreamer's need to see clearly what is happening in the core of some problem or event. They need to see or understand something in greater depth.

Yawning The dreamer needs an outlet so they can escape from a boring situation. Another outlet is needed for their creativity.

Yeast This symbol should reassure the dreamer that if they let nature take its course, expansion and growth will happen.

Yellow The colour yellow in a dream often relates to the dreamer's intellectual thinking process. It points to intelligence, discipline, sincerity, attention to detail and harmony. Dreaming of yellow can symbolise the dreamer's creativity and their need for originality and change. However, it is the colour that relates to fear. This dream should help to heal the dreamer by releasing the tension that blocks their fear, by balancing the emotion with the intellect.

Zodiac To dream of the zodiac suggests that the dreamer feels astrology could be a way of helping them see things from a different perspective.

Zoo This is symbolic of the collection of many different types and races in the world. How does the dreamer feel about that in relation to where they fit in?